TOUCHING
A CHILD'S
HEART

TOUCHING A CHILD'S HEART

An Innovative,
Encouraging Guide
to Becoming a
Good Storyteller

MARY TERESE DONZE, ASC

AVE MARIA PRESS
Notre Dame, Indiana

Library of Congress Catalog Card Number: 85-71557
International Standard Book Number: 0-87793-290-5

Cover design by Elizabeth J. French

Printed and bound in the United States of America

To Jesus Christ
Prince of Storytellers

CONTENTS

Across the fields of yesterday
he sometimes comes to me
a little child just back from play
the child I used to be.
—Thomas S. Jones, Jr.

Just between us . . .

This is not a storyteller's manual even though storytelling techniques are included. Rather, it is an attempt to persuade teachers of religion to use stories in their classes not as an occasional thing but as part of their regular method of conveying the truths they teach. Further, it is an effort to suggest that teachers approach the stories with an acceptance and reverence that allow their own hearts to be changed before they attempt to use the stories with children.

The information in the text that has to do with the telling of stories to children is, in most instances, equally useful in telling stories to adults.

The suggestions given are primarily applicable to a class. You can be more flexible when telling the story to a single child.

Wherever the text speaks of telling a story, the same can usually be said of reading a story. But the preference is for telling rather than reading since a read story is in danger of reaching the listeners without first passing through the heart of the storyteller.

An annotated list of stories or books of reference follows the text. This list is typical rather than lengthy. Choose those that warm the heart. Make them your own and stay with them.

ONCE UPON A TIME

Storytelling is as old as the human race. Somewhere very long ago Mother Eve surely gathered her children about her and told them how "Once upon a time...."

The magic of those words is still with us. Think of how we perk to attention when a speaker says, "That reminds me of the time when . . ." or "Once when I was young. . . ." When others speak of themselves, we sit up and listen, hoping they will reveal themselves to the point where we can more closely relate to them since, until that happens, they remain a closed book, a mystery.

We listen, too, because in the self-revelation of others we hope to find ourselves. In each of us there is something of the other. In you there is part of me. When you speak, I listen to hear that something which is an echo of myself. You are a mirror in which I see myself and in which I am identified with you, in which our deepest relationship is revealed. When I have found how you are my own self and I am you, I have reached the point where love in its truest form is possible between us. It is the place at which "loving the neighbor as yourself" becomes not only possible but inevitable. When I know you, when I find the common ground on which we are one, it would be impossible for me not to love you. And so I listen to you and come to know your inner feelings, your joys, your sorrows, the tenderness that is in you, the beauty, yes, your weaknesses, too, for it is in your joys, your sorrows, your weaknesses, that I find my identity. So I listen to you when you speak of yourself.

And just as I listen to you speak of yourself, I listen when you read or speak to me of another, for in that other I again see myself. In the story you tell me I see how another copes with problems, meets disappointments, attains final victory.

We don't make enough use of stories in helping one another. Yet it was our Lord's method. In the fourth chapter of Mark, verse 34, we read that "he did not speak to them without a parable."

Most people shy away from the explicit telling

of stories because they consider it a waste of time. And it is. But what a glorious waste of time. In this sense storytelling is related to prayer — contemplation— and love. Unless we are willing to waste time with the Lord or with loved ones, we are going to miss the profound beauty and wonder of a meaningful experience. We can't pray and count off the minutes at the same time. At least we shouldn't. Neither can we relate lovingly to another with our eyes on the clock. Cinderella, forgetting to watch the time when she was with the Prince, is a classic example of how time loses its significance when we are in the presence of the beloved.

It is the same with storytelling. There must be a leisurely abandonment to the now. No rush. No hurry. Just a peaceful and total awareness of the present.

In
the
beginning
was
the
Word

—John 1:1

HOW TO BEGIN

The stories you choose to tell will depend on the listeners, on their age, their experience. Feel out the group. Know the message you want to get across, and tell it when the time is psychologically ripe—when both you and your listeners are ready for it.

As a general rule use stories that focus on love, beauty, adventure, courage, laughter. And don't hesitate to tell stories that bring children to tears of wonder and awe in the presence of the noble and good.

Begin with simple stories, especially if you are telling rather than reading the story. Find tales that begin with quick, direct involvement of the main character, develop along clear, strong lines, explode into a vivid climax, and come to a swift but satisfying close.

The heart has its reasons

—Blaise Pascal

WHY TELL STORIES?

1) Ordinarily we tell (or listen to) stories for the pure joy they afford. A good story needs no excuse except that it is—just as mountain climbers climb for no other reason than that the mountain is there. That as religion teachers we tell the story to get across a religious truth should in no way detract from the joy in the story itself.

2) Stories nourish the imagination. A small child usually has a highly developed imagination and can play for hours with an invisible playmate. So long as the child confines the imaginings to a world of fantasy, most adults consider them harmless and smile at the vagaries. As the child grows older, the fantasies begin to conflict with the real world. At times the two are confused and adults call those confusions lies. In sheer self-defense the child learns to adjust to things as they are. In proportion, as reali-

ty is accepted, the imaginary world begins to recede. For some children, as they grow older, the land of the imagination fades and never returns. Or, if at times it does encroach on their everyday living, they thrust it behind them as something they need to shed along with their childhood. Stories help bring the imagination back into play.

3)   Telling stories to children is one of the most effective ways of motivating them to read. A child who has sat on the lap of a father or mother and listened to the parent lift all those marvelous tales from the pages of the story book will naturally want to be initiated into the mystery of reading. That child is truly poor who has never learned, long before the age for school, the magic of the printed word.

4)   Stories also set up ideals for children. There is in each of us a natural desire to strive toward a goal, to want to achieve. Good stories furnish worthwhile goals. Listening to a story completely changed the lives of Saint Augustine and Saint Francis. This is true of countless others. Think back in your own life on how you have been influenced by a good book, a story.

5)   Stories are also sources of self-revelation. They help us see ourselves as others see us. Children may not recognize or admit their limitations. A story

may give them the opportunity to study someone who struggles with those same limitations and to learn how to handle them. In her book, *The Way of the Storyteller*, Ruth Sawyer has a charming tale of Wee Meg Barnileg who was an *enfant terrible*. How little Meg learns to become loving and unselfish is an easy lesson for any child to follow.

6) The storyteller is given the opportunity to help children retain or recover their sense of wonder. The most ordinary things become objects of fascination for young children. A baby will suddenly one day be completely taken up with the discovery of its toes. How many times since you and I were infants have we looked at our toes and marveled at them? We should. They are masterpieces of anatomy. But we've lost our sense of wonder.

Child...
thy
smile
will
surely
hail
the
love-gift
of a
fairy
tale

—Lewis Carroll

THE CASE FOR FAIRY TALES

For years fairy tales were relegated to the nursery. Now it is becoming increasingly evident that they are a delightful way of teaching gospel values. Many of these tales make a point more quickly and forcibly and altogether more pleasurably than any amount of dry theorizing.

Suppose a child is discouraged, disheartened, feels there is nothing going for him or her; let that child listen to the story of "The Ugly Duckling." If he or she needs to be taught about humility, about the importance of being lowly of heart, tell the tale of "King Thrush-Beard," a story about a proud princess whose father married her to a beggar to cure her of her haughtiness. After learning to live humbly with her beggar-husband, the princess discovers that he is the young king she had once spurned. Only when she realizes how unworthy she is of his goodness does she understand what her pride had done to her. In the King's brushing aside her past ingratitude, we see God's forgiving love and munificent manner of rewarding us beyond our desserts, even beyond our wildest dreams. In many ways fairy tales show us how the gospel is worked out in day-to-day living.

If the child needs to learn the value of truth, tell the story of "The Emperor's New Clothes." You will not need to ask for a reaction to the story. The tale itself will cause questioning in the child's own heart: Would I have pretended to see the clothes because I did not have the courage to say what I thought was true?

Suppose you are speaking to the child of how cooperation with grace makes the soul ever more sensitive to the whisperings of the Holy Spirit. Tell the story of "The Princess and the Pea." No one but a genuine princess, delicately reared, would have felt a pea under 20 mattresses. In the same way only those tuned to the things of God will hear the Spirit speaking to their hearts.

Don't draw these conclusions for the children. Draw all the conclusions in your presentation of the class material. Then you might say, as you move into your story, "And that reminds me of...." When the story ends, let it stand on its own.

Fairy tales are also related to the gospels in that they teach the same topsy-turvy morality. Where, for example, is the justice (according to our "reasonable" way of thinking and judging) in giving the same wages to a man who worked only one hour as to another who worked the entire day? Yet the gospels approve of this. Or who would risk the fate of 99 sheep to save one, and a rascally one at that? Or, again, who would expect to save his or her life by losing it?

But some would argue that the good things in fairy tales come too easily, that fairy stories encourage children to think they can get something for nothing. That is a mistaken notion. The magic of fairy tales is not a give-away treasure. The prize is always conditioned by an "if" that demands a struggle. He will win the hand of the princess if he slays the dragon; or, he will win her hand if he finds the answer to the riddle.

The princesses and princes themselves are symbolic figures. In many tales the princess is held captive, locked in a castle by an enemy, waiting to be rescued. That princess is each one of us. She is our true self, exiled in a foreign land, waiting to be liberated by Prince Charming and taken from bondage into a land of happiness and freedom. Our task is to cooperate with the Prince, to "let down our hair" from the tower, to preserve the glass slipper that identifies us as the princess who came to the ball. We are also princes in disguise. An enemy has usurped our dignity by changing us into bears, frogs, swans or deer. We need the touch of love to break the spell that holds us captive.

So many fairy tales have as their theme a quest undertaken by three sons of a king or three brothers. And always it is the youngest son, the one thought most unlikely to win, who comes out victorious. Again, the supernatural irony of the gospels. We are that youngest son, and we should know we are in good company: David was a youngest son, the judge Gideon was the "least important" in his family, Joseph of Egypt was a younger and an unpopular sibling.

The idea of our royal dignity is strong in the fairy tales; and it suggests a challenge to find our true selves, to work with our liberator toward releasing us from the bonds that hold us in subjection and slavery.

**I
am
going
to
speak
to
you
in
parable**

—Psalm 78:2

USING BIBLE STORIES

The bible is an excellent source of stories. The Old Testament is filled with them. Think, for example, of David and Goliath, of Daniel in the lion's den, of the three young men in the fiery furnace. Think of Ruth, of Esther, of Judith.

In the New Testament the dramatic stories—other than the parables—may seem less numerous, but they are there, waiting to be discovered and explored. Try to find these stories behind the bare gospel account. Take the story of the multiplication of the loaves and fishes. Surely there has to be something behind the fact that one little boy had five loaves of bread and two fish when apparently no one else had brought along anything to eat. Where was this little fellow going with all that food? From where had he come?

Or, what of the woman who for 18 years suffered from an infirmity that bent her face to the ground as she walked? Listen to that woman relate her story. Hear her tell of all the years that she suffered, the trouble she had in making clothes fit: always the need to have them cut short in front to keep her from stumbling and longer in the back to make allowance for her stooped condition.

Then Jesus comes along. Hear him question her about her infirmity. Listen to those healing words that make her a normal, upright woman again.

None of us has difficulty recognizing and accepting the miracle. "God is wonderful in all his works," we exclaim. But at times we miss the human element, the thing that happened after the miracle, the thing the evangelists did not record but which could often make the gospel character more human, more real, more close to us. If we stay with just what the gospel tells us, we may miss much of what Christ meant to the persons with whom he related.

The gospel doesn't tell us, but surely when the woman with the crooked back stood upright, cured and whole once more, her dress must have gone up in front and dragged in back. See her happiness and embarrassment all caught up in one great triumph of resourcefulness as she snatches the shawl from her shoulders and makes it serve as an apron to cover her exposed legs. No big issue, but a human experience that must have brought from Jesus an approval of her swift ingenuity.

Or, think of Mary, the mother of Jesus, on the night after Jesus' death. Think of how she relived his passion, of how she missed him, yearned for him. And then be there when she sees him alive and radiant and glorious at the dawn of that first Easter Day.

Always go beyond the story as it is given in the gospels. Keep away from improbable fantasies, but remember that the people in the scripture stories were people like you and me who responded emotionally to others in much the same way as we do. Look for those personal reactions in the gospel. It is of these human qualities that true "story" is made.

An
old
story...
the
glory
of
it
is
forever

—Virgil

OTHER STORIES

Many stories besides fairy tales and biblical accounts can convey religious values to the young. We might effectively use H.G. Wells' story, "The Country of the Blind," or Helen Keller's "Three Days to See" to help children appreciate the wonder of the gift of sight. Or, to make them aware of the great blessing of hearing, we could relate the story of Beethoven, a man who loved music and spent his life putting together beautiful sounds yet lived with deafness.

Then there is the story of Glenn Cunningham to make us grateful that we can walk and run and jump. Glenn's is also a story of moral courage. When he was a boy, Glenn burned his legs so badly in a fire that the doctors said he would never walk again. Glenn not only relearned to walk but to run. He held the record for the world's fastest mile in 1938, and in the 1936 Olympics he won the silver medal for the 1500 meter race.

To stress the goodness of the Lord, "Footprints" is a tender and moving story of God's loving care, and it is simple enough to be understood even by the very young.

One night a man had a dream. He dreamed he was walking along the beach with the Lord. Across the sky flashed scenes from his life. In each scene he noticed two sets of footprints in the sand: one belonging to him and the other to the Lord.

When the last scene of his life flashed before him, he looked back at the footprints in the sand. He noticed that many times along the path of his life there was only one set of footprints. He also noticed that it happened at the very lowest and saddest times in his life.

This really bothered him and he questioned the Lord about it. "Lord, you said that once I decided to follow you, you'd walk with me all the way. But I have noticed that during the most troublesome times in my life, there is only one set of footprints. I don't understand why, when I needed you most, you would leave me."

The Lord replied, "My precious, precious child. I love you and I would never leave you. During your times of trial and suffering, when you see only one set of footprints, it was then that I carried you" (Author unknown).

Begin to make a file of stories that carry a message you want to pass on to your listeners, a message of beauty, a noble ideal, a worthwhile goal. The daily media fill our minds with the drab, the sordid, the violent. If we are to have courage to rise above all this and to strive for the heights, we need to be encouraged by stories of the brave, the reverent, the loving.

We need not always tell or read the story. We should challenge our listeners to discover their own stories. The following reflection, though not a story, shows how we live in a world of wonder with story elements all about us.

I am seated in my room. All about me is darkness except for the faint circle of light made by a small candle that flickers here before me on my desk.

I relax in the chair. I am aware of my breath coming and going, deep and rhythmic. All the while I focus my eyes on the candle before me, the wax, the wick, the flame.

There is nothing else on the desk. I reach out and let the fingers of both my hands encircle the candle, touch it, hold it lightly.

33

I look into the flame. Slowly, noiselessly, it opens up. I see a field of clover. The sun shines brightly on the blossoms. I smell the sweet fragrance of the purple flowers. A farmer, who has a name as personal to himself as my name is to me, planted that field. I see him now, turning the sod, scattering the seed, watching the skies, hoping, rejoicing in thankfulness for the blessing of a good crop. I do not know this farmer, but his life is touching mine. From his field of clover, bees drew the nectar that formed the honey in the wax comb from which my candle was made.

I see the bees. I hear their drowsy humming. I watch with what fine precision they form the comb. A world of wisdom opens up to me in their instinctive action. They, too, are part of my candle.

Then there were those who gathered the wax, people I will never know. People with joys and sorrows I can never share. Tired people maybe, underpaid people. People with cares at home, sick children, leaky roofs. People with rent to pay and no money to pay it. Or maybe happy people, people who sang as they worked. Their labor has made this candle possible for me.

34

In the factory many hands were active to form this wax into candles. Some ran the machinery, some packed the finished product. All stand before me now, placing this candle into my curled fingers.

And the wick. Not long ago it was part of a boll of fiber growing in a cotton field. Was it picked by hand? By someone whose back ached from hours of work? It, too, went through many channels before it came to me.

I continue to look at this small candle on my desk. I bought it last Christmas. I picked it from dozens of other candles. People had passed by it day after day, lifted it, considered buying it, laid it back on the counter. That morning in December I found it, liked it, bought it. I became another link with all that had gone into the history of its candleness. Now it burns before me.

Minutes before, I struck a match to light this candle. What mystery, too, in that match head. A small gray blister on the tip of a narrow strip of cardboard, it carries the power to start a conflagration that might level a city, a forest, or blow up a mountain. Now it bursts into a tiny blaze and, without diminishing itself, gives a flame to my candle.

How real, yet undefinable, that flame! Its movement. Its color. The need for air it shares with me. I watch the melting wax feed the wick and see the flame consume and transform them both. Soon this candle will disappear, only to continue in its entirety in another form. What mystery in this small taper.

I touch this slender wax cylinder with new respect. All creation is contained in it: people, plants, inanimate nature. This candle, for which I paid but a few coins, comes to me as a tiny cosmos, a miracle of my workaday life.

And now I pause. I feel mystery gathering about me everywhere—in the wooden chair on which I sit, the pencil with which I will later write, the shoes I am wearing, my glasses, the water I drink, the air that sustains me. In spirit I walk through the great temple of creation. I feel a kinship with everything—the watch on my wrist, the tufts of grass in the cracks of the sidewalk, the moth that flies about my candle flame.

O God, open my eyes yet more to the world of mystery in which I live. Let me know awe in its presence. Make me gentle in its use. And grant me never to touch with irreverent hand or thought the gifts about me. Amen.

That was only a candle. Think what might be done with a chair, a bed, or some part of the body, the eye, the ear. There is no end to the stories that are around us. Once the listeners have had their eyes opened to see all this, they will have had restored to them—perhaps in an even fuller way—the sense of wonder they may have lost.

A

**verse
may
find
him
who
a
sermon
flies**

—George Herbert

POETRY AS STORY

In using stories to reach children we should not overlook the possibilities in poetry. Poems often have great story value and for some occasions may be more effective than prose.

At the same time a poem demands more care in its choice. You may want to use recognized literary works. There is a broad field from which to choose, both in religious and profane literature. However, occasionally you may find that some simple verse, some rhyming lines on a leaflet, would be more helpful. Don't hesitate to use them. Grace is not necessarily linked to works of genius. I clipped this verse from a Catholic tabloid years ago and have used it from time to time with young people:

May I always love life
As I love it today

When with faith and with courage
I start on my way.
No fear for the future
That stretches ahead,
No past years regretting,
No dreams that are dead.
May the years in their passing
My standards uphold.
To the ideals of youth
May I cling when I'm old.
Toward the far heights of greatness
I've set for my soul,
May I steadily climb
Though I ne'er reach the goal.

With the very young, choose a poem as if you were selecting a toy for the child. Let it be something simple and warm and loving, as you might choose a bubble pipe or a teddy bear or a rag doll rather than something more elaborate.

The poems you use need not be narrative. They need not tell a story as we commonly think of story. But they must reveal that human element that makes either story or poem a happy medium for heart to speak to heart. The important thing is: Can you and the child meet in this poem?

If you choose to read or recite a poem for the group, practice reading it, just as you would with a story, no matter how short the poem is. You will find it substantially more difficult to communicate effectively through poetry than through prose. Part of this difficulty comes through not being able to put the poem into your own words. This should not discourage you from using a meaningful poem or verse. But you need to be prepared. You need to be completely at ease with the content of the poem, to have a genuine appreciation of it, to feel untrammeled by its form.

In fact, I am tempted to say that if you can't warm up to poetry in the way mentioned above, don't try using it to reach others. And yet a poem can sometimes operate on its own—just as a story might—regardless of how it is presented. I would not count on it, but I know it is true. It happened to me when I was a child.

I was 11 that year, in the sixth grade, and it was one of those lovely afternoons in late April. I sat at my school desk, a book open before me, my mind wandering. Outside the classroom window the world brimmed with life and beauty.

When I dared, I raised my eyes from the book and looked out. The forsythia bushes down near the school yard fence were brilliant with blossoms. The tall, new grass lay with the wind, looking slick and glassy in the sunlight. From somewhere a jay screamed.

Then the teacher's desk bell jangled, calling out the time for reading class. I filed forward with the other girls from the row by the window, and we took our places along the blackboard wall, the tips of our shoes duly touching the chalkline on the floor.

Our lesson for the day was Thomas Moore's poem, "The Meeting of the Waters." I must have prepared it the evening before. I can't remember. But when it came my turn, I read aloud:

> Sweet Vale of Avoca! How calm could I rest
> In thy bosom of shade, with the friends I love
>   best:
> Where the storms that we feel in this cold world
>   would cease
> And our hearts, like thy waters, be mingled in
>   peace.

How it was then, I don't know, but the magic of those words suddenly held me, and for one breathless moment I was in that faraway valley, wrapped in its peace. I felt shot through with a wild joy, a delicious pain. Then the moment passed, and I was back in the classroom.

I was only a child at the time, teetering on my

last tomboy days, but that poem did something to me, became a religious experience for me, and it did it without any apparent effort of the teacher. So, while it is important that you make a genuine attempt to prepare well each story or poem you use in your religion class, it is also important to remember that the results are not necessarily proportionate to your efforts, nor do they always appear at a place where you might expect them. Here it was in a reading class, and the input of the teacher was insignificant. Yet the effect on me was lasting.

What will a child learn sooner than a song

—Alexander Pope

SONG IN STORYTELLING

When we tell a story or read a poem to children, we involve their minds and hearts; when our story or poem is set to music, we engage also their bodies. Think of how a few bars of music set feet tapping. It is as if somewhere within each of us there is a silent instrument waiting for a rhythmic beat that will cause its strings to vibrate.

Music also induces a mood. If the sounds, joined to the rhythm, are beautiful, the mood is one that opens us to the noble and generous. Wild sounds can devastate us.

It is this emotional stimulus in music that prepares the heart to respond to the message of the lyrics. An 8-year fugitive from justice stepped into a theater one afternoon when a religious service was being held. He had come to listen to the music. When the vast assembly sang the hymn, "Nearer, my God, to Thee," the man left the theater, weeping bitterly. The following morning he turned himself in to the authorities. Had someone simply read the lyrics, it is doubtful whether he would have been so moved. But the music triggered his emotions.

And it is good that we listen to our emotions. Not too many years ago the emotions were looked upon as the Cinderellas of the spiritual life. The mind and will were to be fixed on God. The feelings were suspect and frowned upon. Now we know that unless the spiritual life touches on the whole person—body, soul, mind, imagination, feeling—the untouched areas may be lost to the enemy.

Besides their emotional appeal, song-stories have other advantages. Often they are retained for years in their complete and accurate form. While it has nothing to do with a religious theme, I can still recall from my childhood a song-story about the wreck of the dirigible Shenandoah that was destroyed by a storm. A further advantage to the use of song-stories is that children often carry the songs from the classroom into their everyday world.

Select song-stories with as much care as you exercise in choosing other stories. Have a few choice selections that become special to you and your group. If you are able to sing well, you may want to sing these songs to your class. I would advise against it. Put the song on tape so that both you and your group can listen to it without the distractions attendant on listening to live singing. It's the song and its message that is important, not the singer.

If you do not have a reasonably good singing voice, look for prepared tapes. There are many good ones on the market today, and you are certain to find a few that will fit into your program. Play them for yourself until they become part of you before you present them to your group.

I would suggest that you don't take time out to teach the songs to the children. Expose the group to each song by having them listen to it on enough meaningful occasions that they will pick up the words and melody much as they do with songs they hear on television or over the radio. Neither would I have them sing along with the voice on the tape. Hum? Yes, if they do it spontaneously and softly since the humming will fix the melody in their minds.

Here, as with poetry, the song-stories need not be narrative. Some of them will be, such as songs that give the Christmas story. Others may suggest a story, like the Negro spiritual "Were You There?" Still others may be on themes that you are currently using in the religion class.

Keep your song-stories few and special. With careful timing, your few stories, poems, songs, will slowly pass from your heart into the hearts of your listeners.

...Delighting and instructing at the same time

—Horace

HINTS FOR STORYTELLERS

Storytelling is an art. Not everyone can become expert at it. But we can learn to follow certain guidelines that will make us more effective storytellers.

1) Know the vocabulary level of your audience. There is no sense in reading or telling a story filled with words that are unfamiliar to the listeners. This is particularly important when the unfamiliar word is a key to the understanding or mental visualization of the story. When a child pictures a ship rearing on end and "bowing," because you read about the bow of a ship and he or she knows only one meaning for the word "bow," the ship story will lose some of its effectiveness.

Sometimes you may unwittingly use an unfamiliar word. If it is not in a child's vocabulary, you can be sure the child will pull it into his or her frame of reference and make it fit in with what is already known. At times this may not make a significant change in the overall effect of the story, but it is best to be aware of the listeners' vocabulary level.

When a friend of mine was a child, she heard the grownups singing this line in a song, "And those that sneer will be the first to cheer...." The word "sneer" was foreign to her, but she sang along "And those that's near...." What she understood and sang made some kind of sense to her.

2) Take care not to go off on a tangent when you are telling a story. If the main character wore socks of different colors, it would be in line to mention it if the fact had something to do with forwarding the story. But there's no need to give the entire history of the socks before proceeding. Use only such digressions as are called for by the plot.

3) Avoid inserting too many details. If you are telling a story which involves the removal of 100 crystal marbles from one jar to another, you wouldn't think of saying, "And he took out one marble, and then the second, and then the third...." Keep in mind what was said before: Use only such details or take in only such side issues as are necessary for the story's development.

4) Hold to the facts in the story. This is par-

ticularly true of biographical material. If the hero was less than virtuous, don't gloss over the fact. Let the listeners know the good and the bad. Many stories of the saints have been ruined by the hagiographer's failing to include the human frailties of the saints. If the listeners are unable to handle the element of evil, they are not yet ready for the story.

5) Don't "water down" the story in an effort to lower it to the language of a group of listeners. This would be like telling the story of the temptation of Christ in the desert and changing Jesus' "Begone, Satan!" to "Get going, Old Nick!" A love for the finer, nobler things is not developed by settling for the cheap and shoddy. Do make adaptations where necessary, but also try to lift the minds of your listeners. Make them reach to what is beyond them. This is the secret of growth.

6) Don't "show and tell" at the same time. It may destroy the effect of your story. Have you ever attended a class or lecture where the speaker began by passing out flyers and kept talking while they were distributed? If what the speaker was saying was an important announcement, chances are that half the group did not hear what was said and then missed hearing the next thing by whispering to find out what the first announcement was.

If you plan to use pictures in telling your story, either show the pictures beforehand or stop in the proper place in the story and present the pictures. Allow the listeners time to study and enjoy them, but remove them once you begin telling the story again. Most people attend better when an appeal is make to them through one sense at a time. It's like closing your eyes or sitting in a dark room while listening to something. Each sense seems sharper by being used alone. This may account for the tradition of telling tales around the fireplace where everyday realities seem to recede into the dark, and the now and here are all that matter.

7)   Resist the urge to encourage the listeners to collaborate with the telling of the story. "And what do you think happened next?" asks the storyteller. The answer may be a far-fetched absurdity; but, if the one giving the answer has peer influence, the class may take off on the new tangent and completely derail the story.

8)   Do not have the children dramatize the stories you tell them. Some storytellers want their listeners to act out what they have heard. They use the "learning of lines" as a vocabulary builder. Do this with stories the children make up or with some stories from their readers. But the stories you tell should be special stories, classics for the heart. So

little of genuine loveliness comes into our lives that we should be loath to force that little into serving the practical. To do so is to demand that a princess become a scullery maid because a maid gets something done.

9) Discourage attempts to illustrate your story. If you have good pictures, use them as suggested above; otherwise let mental pictures be enough. The reasoning is the same as for not dramatizing the story. How could the children satisfactorily illustrate, for example, the story of Peter Pan? How could they capture the elusive presence and charming audacity of Peter or the fragile beauty of Tinker Bell?

But what if a child asks to draw a picture of what he or she has heard? If you can't avoid the situation, refrain from commenting on the drawing while affirming the child's effort. Marie Shedlock, in her book *The Art of the Story-Teller*, relates how a little boy spontaneously volunteered to draw the picture of a knight about whom the teacher had told a story. After a few trials at the chalkboard, the child stood back from his drawing and regarded it with a frown. Then he turned to the teacher and admitted with real concern that somehow he could not get the knight to look right. Most children are surprisingly good critics of their own artistic creations.

Pictures in general fall short as illustrations for stories. This holds true even for adult stories. Notice how few pictures appear in modern novels. A picture on the cover to lure you to reading, but after that—nothing. Some people even refuse to attend a movie based on a story they love because they are afraid that the pictures they see will not be those they carry in their minds.

10) Cultivate a healthy rapport with your class before you begin to use stories. If the children feel you are displeased with them, aren't interested in them, don't love them, they will instinctively resist any effort you make to instruct them, and your best stories will fall flat. Once they sense that you really care for them, you can lead them anywhere.

11) Resist the temptation to tell a story that comes to mind on the spur of the moment when you are teaching. If it is a good story and applies, it is worth being thought through and used when you review the present material. Don't ruin a good story by telling it when you are unprepared even though you think you remember it well. Remembering isn't all there is to storytelling.

12) Recognize that some stories are not suitable for you to tell. You may like them and want to use them, but you either lack the personality to

tell them well, or the voice quality, perhaps even the personal appearance. If you feel strongly about the stories and want the class to hear them, you might get someone to read them onto a tape for you.

13)   Know your story well so that you can concentrate on how you tell it. Again, this is not a bid for dramatics. Sincerity and simplicity are quite enough. But one dramatic device that enriches even sincerity and simplicity is the wise use of the pause.

Part of the last sentence in my book, *The Kingdom Lost and Found*, is "...somebody somewhere was whispering, 'I love you!'" The emotional impact of the sentence, the impact of the entire story, is lost if the reader fails to pause before the last three words. In that slight but significant pause, something transpires that is difficult to analyze. Whether it is the sudden effect of the moment of silence or the instantaneous flow and ebb of expectancy, whatever it is, that pause creates an atmosphere that gives the words "I love you" a dimension of infinity. Read the sentence with the pause and then without it, and you will understand what I mean.

14)   Refrain from analyzing the story for your listeners. "But," you object, "I want to be sure they got the message." You needn't worry. A good story

needs no one to explain it. Jesus himself acted on this principle. He ended a story with, "He who has ears to hear, let him hear" (Mk 4:9). In other words, "Get out of this what you can." Only when the apostles pressed him for an explanation did Christ reveal the meaning of his parables to them.

A story reveals a truth. It also disguises it. To those ready for the revelation, the truth will be evident. From those who are not strong enough to bear the truth, it will be mercifully withheld. Christ said to his apostles, "I have yet many things to say to you, but you cannot bear them now" (Jn 16:12).

If you try to explain the meaning of your story, those who got less from it than what you explain will be confused. The story will lose its force and pleasure for them. For those who got more from the story than your explanation covers, you will narrow their horizons and minimize the treasure they found.

15) Do not look for tangible results. Storytelling is a two-way endeavor. You may have the greatest collection of stories in the world, and you may be an accomplished storyteller, but ordinarily you have no sure way of knowing how your stories are getting across to your listeners. If you are speaking to very young children, you can usually get their honest reaction through their attention or lack of

it. But even with them, you may never know, or you may learn only years later, how much a certain story influenced their lives. The storyteller casts a pebble into the child's heart-pool, and the ripples move out in ever-widening circles. Someday, somewhere, one of your listeners may be moved to accomplish the noble, the heroic, the near-impossible because of a story heard as a child.

When you are telling stories to older children you may have to keep up your enthusiasm by blowing on your own fires. Often the reactions of older listeners surface in inverse proportion to the effect the story has made on them. If they are profoundly moved, they may sit with passive, noncommittal expressions. You may feel they are bored and apathetic. The truth may be that they are so touched by the story that they feel the need to mask their true feelings.

Respect all these responses, but do not measure the success of your story by the apparent indifference of the listeners. If your story was good and you loved it and gave it all you had, you have succeeded. You are, after all, only the sower. Drop the seed and move on to other fields. Time and God's grace will foster the growth. You may not be around to witness it, but good has been done. What greater reward could you ask?

The
world
is
charged
with
the
grandeur
of
God

—Gerard Manley Hopkins

THE STORYTELLER'S ENVIRONMENT

Most public libraries employ a trained storyteller, and books are written to help these storytellers become effective at their job. You may find some of these books helpful. At the same time it is important for you as a religious educator to remember that you have a different primary purpose in telling stories. You are deliberately trying to strengthen the impact of a moral or religious precept. This does not mean that you should be less careful in choosing and presenting your story. It does mean that you do not arrange a physical setting for the story and have the listeners come with the idea "Teacher is going to tell us a story today." Your stories flow as a natural follow-up on some religious truth you are trying to reinforce.

Nevertheless, some effective storytelling techniques may be helpful to know.

1)   Do not wear jewelry or a type of clothing that calls attention to itself and away from what you are saying.

2)   Maintain the same sitting or standing posture throughout the entire story.

3)   If you are reading from a book, lower it enough that the children are able to see your entire face.

4)   Avoid the over-dramatic. Too much gesturing or facial gymnastics become artificial and again focus attention on you instead of on what you say. A good storyteller's voice and eyes are so expressive that he or she needs very little gesticulating and grimacing.

5)   Have a general idea of the type of stories that appeal to your age group. Very young children prefer stories about familiar objects. They easily accept animals that talk and delight in stories that have repetitive lines. Children from first to fourth grades enjoy fairy tales, myths, fables, folklore. Fifth- to seventh-graders are intrigued by mystery stories, biographies of boys and girls their own age, and stories of travel. After the seventh grade children's interests reflect their growing maturity, They then look for books about adventure, sports, romance, science, history, lives of great men and women.

It is good for you to know the reading interests of children of different ages, but it should in no way hamper your freedom in selecting a story for use in religion class. If a fairy tale makes your point, use it with any grade level. The way you tell the story will determine its effectiveness. What I am trying to say is that you should not omit telling a good story just because it was not originally meant for the age group you are teaching. Tell the story in your own words, adapting it to your listeners. It would not be that hard to tell a 6-year-old about "The Country of the Blind" even though it was written for adults. Little children are refreshingly open to truth and often astound us by the profundity of their perceptions.

This
above
all:
to
thine
own
self
be
true

—William Shakespeare

THE STORYTELLER

When we teach the truth, we speak to the head of the child; when we support the teaching of the truth with a related story, we beat a path to the child's heart. And just as the knowledge we teach passed through our minds, our heads, before we were qualified to transfer it to the child, the story, too, if it is to be effective, must have gone through our hearts.

Try not to think of the story as something added to the substance of the instruction. The story may well be the only reason the child remembers the truth you set out to teach. Approach the story, therefore, with something of the same awe and reverence that you bring to things of the spirit. To do this, it is not enough that you tell the story, even that you tell it well. You must love it.

Think about the story long before you use it. Live with the characters of your story, especially with the main ones. Talk with them, feel and think with them. Know why they act as they do. Let them become real for you, people you know, people about whom you feel concern.

Only when the story comes alive for you, is part of you, gets into your blood stream, are you ready to fruitfully share it with another. It will then no longer be "just another story." It will be your self-revelation in which children can discover their own identity and feel at one with you in a warm and intuitive relationship. You will have reached their hearts because you will have vicariously revealed your own.

Develop a love for words and you will have no difficulty telling stories as they need to be told. Regard all word with reverence, not only the words you use in prayer or those in your religion text, but all words wherever they appear. Words have a mysterious power. They can raise up or cast down, encourage or damn.

Stop now and sit somewhere, alone, with a book. Any book will do. Read aloud, slowly, one short paragraph. Pronounce each word fully, no sloppiness, no slurring. Use your lips. Relish each word as if you tasted it, smelled it, touched it. Try to see the individual words with new eyes. Let the power that they hold grow on you.

Better still, listen to Carey Landry's "Lay Your Hands Gently upon Me" or "I Will Never Forget you." Words become sacramentals on his lips. No word, however insignificant its role in the sentence, is passed over in a perfunctory or slipshod manner. Landry gives each word a presence, a nowness, that, regardless of how it is combined with others to express the thought, makes the isolated word a thing of beauty in itself.

Modern emphasis on the value of speed reading has made us lose sight of the loveliness of individual words. We read in much the same way as many people eat, wolfing down their food because they have something else to do. As if eating were not also something to do, a very human activity and therefore worthy of being done in a human way.

Eat slowly, read slowly, with a reverence for each morsel, for each word, and you will find that a certain power and peace come to you with each mouthful you eat and each word you read. All of which is nothing else but an affirmation of the old Latin adage *Age quod agis*— do what you are doing. Give full time to each action. It isn't what we do, it's that we do it and how we do it that makes us better humans. Learn to do this by beginning with a new and deliberate approach to your reading. The stories you tell will then renew you at the same time as they form the minds of those you teach.

In this personal renewal effort, read some stories solely for your own benefit. It sounds unorthodox—and traditional religious practice will scarcely suggest it—but try using a fable or fairy tale during your next meditative prayer period. You might very well begin with the Grimm Brothers' tale, "Hans in Luck." The story is an example of the connection between inner freedom gained by detachment and true happiness. Hans, the hero of the tale, is apparently of less than average intelligence, and the story is absurd, including the title. In fact, it is precisely the incongruous title that betrays the deeper significance of the story. Hans is lucky because he is unlucky. Again, the foolishness of the gospels.

> Hans had served his master for seven years, and at the end of that time Hans said, "Master, the time I pledged to serve you is up. I should like to go home to my mother. Please may I have my wages?"

> His master replied, "You have served me faithfully and honestly, Hans, for seven long years, and as your service was, so shall be your reward."

> With these words, he gave Hans a lump of gold as big as his head. Hans took his handkerchief from his pocket, wrapped the gold in it,

swung it over his shoulder and set out on the road toward his home village. The big lump of gold bumped and thumped against his shoulder and he began to wish it were not so heavy.

As he walked along, a horseman came in sight. He trotted along gaily on a fine animal.

"Ah!" said Hans aloud. "What a fine thing riding is! That one is seated, as it were, upon a chair, while I must walk in the dust lugging this lump of gold."

The rider, overhearing the word "gold" and recognizing Hans as a foolish fellow, said slyly, "If you like, we can exchange. I will give you my horse, and you can give me your lump of gold."

"With all my heart," cried Hans. "But I will tell you fairly that you are undertaking a heavy burden."

The man dismounted before Hans could change his mind, took the gold, and helped Hans onto the horse. Giving him the reins, he said, "Now, when you want to go faster, just cluck with your tongue and cry, "Gee up! Gee up!"

Hans was delighted when he found himself on the horse, riding along so gaily with no burden to carry. After a while he thought he should like to go faster. So he cried, "Gee up!

Gee up!" as the man had told him. Off went the horse at a hard trot, and before Hans knew what he was about, he was thrown head over heels into a ditch.

The horse would have run off if he had not been stopped by a peasant who came along just then, driving a cow before him. Hans picked himself up, shook his fist at the horse, and said angrily, "I will never ride that animal again! Who could want such a prankish nag? Owning a cow is much more sensible. With a cow you can have milk, butter and cheese every day. Ah! What I wouldn't give for a cow!"

"Well," said the peasant, "I will exchange my cow for your prankish horse."

Hans was delighted at the bargain, and so was the peasant. He quickly gave Hans the cow and, swinging himself upon the horse, rode off in a hurry.

Now Hans drove his cow steadily before him.

As soon as he came to an inn, he halted, and with great satisfaction ate all the lunch he had brought with him. After this he again drove his cow along the road in the direction of his mother's village. As the day grew hotter and hotter, Hans became very thirsty.

"This will never do," he thought. "I will milk my cow, and refresh myself." He tied her to a tree, and having no pail, placed his cap below. But try as he would, he could not get a drop of milk. The impatient cow gave him such a kick on the head that he tumbled to the ground. Hans lay in the dirt, holding his head and moaning.

Soon a butcher came along pushing a wheelbarrow in which there was a young pig.

"What on earth has happened?" he exclaimed, helping poor Hans to his feet; and Hans told him all that had occurred. The butcher then said, "Your cow will never give any milk. She is an old beast, and is only good for the butcher!"

"Oh! Oh!" said Hans, pulling his hair over his eyes. "Who would have thought it? I have no desire for cow's meat; it is too tough. Now a young pig like yours tastes like something!"

"Well, now," said the butcher, "I will make an exchange and let you have my pig for your cow."

"Heaven reward you for your kindness!" cried Hans, and giving up the cow, he untied the pig from the wheelbarrow.

Hans walked on again, pleased that everything had happened just as he wished.

Presently a boy overtook him, carrying a fine white goose under his arm.

"Good day," said the boy.

"Good day to you," said Hans, and he began to talk about his luck and what profitable exchanges he had made.

The boy told him that he was carrying the goose to a christening feast.

"Just feel how heavy it is," the boy said. "Why, it has been fattened for eight weeks. Whoever gets a bite of this will have to wipe the grease from each side of his mouth!"

"Yes," said Hans, holding it with one hand. "It is heavy, but my pig is no trifle either."

While he was speaking, the boy kept looking about on all sides and shaking his head suspiciously. At length, he broke out, "I wouldn't say much about that pig if I were you. A pig has just been stolen from the mayor, and I am afraid it is that very same pig under your arm. It will be bad for you if anyone catches you."

Honest Hans was thunderstruck, and he exclaimed, "Ah, Heaven help me in this new trouble! You know the neighborhood better than I do and can hide. You take my pig and let me have your goose."

"That will be a risk," replied the boy, "but still I do not wish to be the cause of your having any misfortune." Quickly he drove the pig off by a side path, while Hans walked on toward home with the goose under his arm.

As he came to the last village on his road home, Hans met a knife-grinder seated beside a hedge, whirling his wheel round and singing:

"Scissors and razors and knives I grind;
A sharper fellow is hard to find."

Hans stopped to watch a bit and said, "You appear to have a good business, if I may judge by your merry song."

"Yes," answered the grinder. "A true knife-grinder is a man who always has money in his pocket. But what a fine goose you have. Where did you buy it?"

"I did not buy it at all," said Hans, "but took it in exchange for my pig."

"And where did you get the pig?"

"I exchanged it for my cow, which I exchanged for a horse."

"And the horse?"

"I gave a lump of gold as big as my head for him."

"And the gold?"

"That was my wages for seven years' work."

"I see you have bettered yourself each time you have traded," said the grinder. "But now, if you could hear money rattling in your pocket as you walked, your fortune would surely be made."

"Well, how shall I manage that?" asked Hans.

"You must become a grinder like me. In this trade you need nothing but a grindstone. I will give you a stone for your goose. Are you agreeable?"

"How can you ask me?" said Hans. "Why, I shall be the luckiest man in the world."

"Now," said the grinder, picking up an ordinary stone which lay nearby. "There you have a fine stone. Take it and use it very carefully!"

Hans took the stone and giving the grinder the goose, walked on with a satisfied air.

"I must have been born to a heap of luck," he thought. "Everything happens just as I wish."

Soon, however, he began to feel very tired, and very hungry, too, for he had been on his way since daybreak. At last he felt unable to go any farther with the heavy stone. He sighed deeply and thought what a good thing it would be if he no longer had to carry it.

Just then he noticed a stream flowing nearby. He decided to sit down beside it to rest and refresh himself. He carefully put the stone down and leaned over to scoop up some water in his hand. He pushed the stone a little too far and over it went into the stream with a loud splash. As it sank beneath the water Hans jumped up and clicked his heels for joy. Then he gave thanks that without even trying he had been delivered from his burden.

"There is no other man under the sun as lucky as I am," exclaimed Hans.

And with a light heart he went gaily along until he reached his mother's house.

After you have worked your way prayerfully through "Hans in Luck," you might want to think more about inner freedom and its place in the heart of the religion teacher.

Most of us start out with our hearts burning to set the world on fire for God. But the good we accomplish will be only in direct proportion to our ability to keep possessive hands off any productive results, any success, any personal aggrandizement that follows our apostolic works.

Our freedom of spirit, therefore, our ability to refrain from grasping the good as if it were our own or—on the negative side—of shrinking in fear at the onset of pain is the most valuable gift that we, the storytellers, can give with our stories.

We gain this freedom through the way we handle both pain and joy. See yourself as a wire screen, a bit of meshed metal. Think of pain as a dense smoke cloud billowing toward you. Do not move aside or seek to avoid it. Hold your ground, not stoically, but loosely, gently, with arms open, as it were, to give the cloud free passage. Say to yourself as you allow it to sift through you in its completeness, "It came . . . to pass."

Do the same with joys. We have a tendency to blunt the ecstatic edge of our joys by gathering them to our hearts and holding them fast. We spoil the very things meant to give us happiness. Learn to relax. Draw the fullness from each drop of happiness that comes your way, but allow it to pass beyond you when its time is up. Both pain and joy will then leave behind a residue of peace and strength.

Somewhere in your storytelling, build your own fable, your own story, around these liberating words of the gospel, "It came to pass." Do that, live that, and you should have no trouble reaching children because you will have met them at a level where you and they are one and where communication has become perfect.

You also might want to come back to thinking about words. You might want to dwell on the relationship of words to invisible thought and on the relationship of Christ, the Eternal Word, to the Father. You might want to think of your own word relationship to God's eternal thought of you.

"When I was a child ... I understood as a child. But when I became a man (woman), I put away the things of a child"—at least some of them. Among the things I kept is the remembrance of a quaint classic on the meaning of eternity which I heard from a Catholic nun, Sister Honore, the year I was in the sixth grade, and which has become the basis for my belief that storytelling is one of the most powerful means of touching and training the heart of a child.

At our school, Faerber's *Catechism* was the religion text one swore by—or at. There wasn't a picture in the entire book, nothing but an endless progression of questions and answers.

Perhaps for Sister Honore's sixth grade it was better that way. Had the book been illustrated, or had the implications of each question been spelled out in detail, it is possible that Sister Honore might have just let things be. As it was, she picked up the abstract theological, doctrinal, and moral ideas and threw them, sparkling with life, onto the screens of our minds.

Each of Sister Honore's religion classes followed this pattern: First came the routine question-and-answer phase (a mandate from our old German pastor). After Sister Honore had assured herself that we knew the answers, the stories followed. She had stories for everything: grace, mercy, forgiveness, heaven, hell. It was her eternity story, however, which for me outrated them all.

Until I heard Sister Honore's version, my childhood concept of foreverness had grown out of a discovery I made from a label on a bottle of maple syrup. On the label was a picture of a little girl sitting before a plate filled with pancakes. She was pouring syrup from a bottle on which was a label with a picture of a little girl sitting before a plate filled with pancakes, and *she* was pouring syrup from a bottle on which was a label with a picture of a little girl sitting before a plate filled with pancakes, and *she* .... I couldn't see all the labels because the pictures got smaller and smaller, but I knew they went on forever and ever. I guessed eternity was something like that.

But not Sister Honore's eternity. Instead of shrinking into some microscopic vanishing point, eternity in her hands broadened until it spread right out of time and space. And while it broadened, Sister Honore was swooping her sixth graders right into it.

It would be impossible to retell it in Sister Honore's manner of delivery, but I can recall the story as clearly today as when I first heard it.

Imagine a ball as large as the earth, she began. If each of you started walking at three miles an hour for eight hours a day, it would take you about three years to walk around such a ball. By that time you'd all have been graduated more than a year. (It was evident she expected we'd carry our books along with us.)

Suppose that the same ball was made of brass. That would make it a very solid ball. And then suppose (we supposed easily under the magic of her sincerity) that once in every million years....(Here she paused for a while to allow us time to get the feel of million. Those who were quick at math volunteered it was a thousand thousand years. That helped. Thousand had meaning for us. Within the six years of our educational odyssey most of us had accumulated at least a thousand "lines" for talking in ranks after second bell.) Suppose—she took up the story again—that every million years a bird, sweeping out from nowhere (her hand swept the fantastic bird into our vision), flew past this enormous ball and brushed it with the tip of its wing.

Someday—it would be a very long time— but someday the wear caused by the brush of that stiff wing feather would begin to show. Not after the first few million years. (Of course not; that would mean only a few wing strokes). Not after the first few thousand million years maybe. But perhaps after the millionth million years, if you looked very closely, you would see the hint of a healthy scuff beginning to show on the big ball. It wouldn't be much, but it would prove that, given enough time and a reliable bird, the entire ball could be worn away. (That made sense. Some of us had bicycles and there were places where the paint was worn off just from something rubbing against that part.)

Nobody, she went on, could figure out how long it would take. If we tried, our minds would stagger to think of the ages and ages that would have to pass. But one thing was sure, she said. If there were still a sun to rise and set on the day when that marvelous bird made its last trip, that sun would rise on a mere sniff of brass and set on empty space.

We all had goose pimples by then. And we finally felt we had a handle on what eternity is like. But no, she said, that wasn't at all what eternity was like, because when that little bird would be making its final swipe at that last breath of brass, eternity would then only be beginning slowly to unroll itself as if it hadn't noticed that a great deal of time had already passed.

Best of all, she continued on her theme, we were going to be there when this happened—all of us. Sister Honore was going to be there, and the boy with the thick glasses who sat in the front desk, and the girl nearest the door—the one with the blond curls that I envied—she was going to be there. I was going to be there, too, and all the rest of the kids around me. We were all going to be on the spot, happy with God, in the wonder of that unbelievable endlessness.

Two years later, when I was 13, my father died, and part of me died with him. But in the bewilderment of loss I remembered Sister Honore's eternity. The thought cheered me. I was glad that papa had not spiralled into some fine point of oblivion but that he was still around somewhere with God, waiting for mama and the five of us kids, and that we'd catch up with him sometime, some place, and be happy again together in that long forever.

Stories for Children and Adults

The Fairy Tales of Hans Christian Anderson

Connolly, Myles. *Mister Blue*. New York: Double-day, 1928. A modern St. Francis of Assisi gives a fresh blueprint for living in the freedom of the children of God.

Donze, Mary Terese, ASC. *The Kingdom Lost and Found*. Notre Dame, Ind.: Ave Maria Press, 1982. Through the power of love a courageous and obedient son brings happiness to his estranged father and to the people of the kingdom.

Donze, Mary Terese. *Down Gospel Byways*. Liguori, Mo.: Liguori Publications, 1984. Stories of 18 gospel people and the effect their meeting with Jesus had on their lives.

Donze, Mary Terese. "The Island that Had No Birds," *Highlights for Children*, May, 1978. A little bird risks everything to bring happiness to a people who had never heard a bird sing.

Gallico, Paul. *The Snow Goose*. New York: Alfred A. Knopf, 1941. This story with its poignant message of faith and love has a grace and simple beauty that is timeless.

The Fairy Tales of the Brothers Grimm

Hawthorne, Nathaniel. *The Great Stone Face*. Boston: Houghton, Mifflin. A powerful example of the influence of ideals and attitudes on the formation of character.

Marshall, Catherine. *Christy*. New York: McGraw-Hill, 1967. Nineteen-year-old Christy Huddleston goes to teach school in a depressed and poverty-stricken area of Appalachia. She learns far more than she teaches and matures through learning to love and to accept the love of others.

Nathan, Robert. *A Portrait of Jenny*. New York: Alfred A. Knopf, 1949. The story of a tender love that bridges the boundaries of time and space.

Paulus, Trina. *Hope for the Flowers*. Ramsey, N.J.: Paulist Press, 1972. A delicately told fable celebrating hope.

Saint-Exupery, Antoine de. *The Little Prince.* New York: Harcourt, Brace, Jovanovich, 1943. An enduring classic of a different type of "desert" experience.

Sanchez-Silva, Jose Maria. *Marcelino Pan y Vino.* New York: Oxford University Press, 1961. An infant is abandoned at the gate of a monastery, and the child is brought up by the monks. The little boy's lonely childhood is suddenly transformed one day when he discovers the Man on the Cross in the monastery garret.

Sawyer, Ruth. "Wee Meg Barnileg and the Fairies," *The Way of the Storyteller.* New York: Penguin Books, 1977. The neighbors were in dread whenever naughty Wee Meg came down the street. Someone was sure to suffer from her mischief. How the fairies helped her become a good and loving child makes a charming story.

Silverstein, Shel. *The Giving Tree.* New York: Harper & Row, 1964. The little boy kept taking and taking and was never really satisfied, but the tree gave everything it had and found true happiness.

Williams, Margery. *The Velveteen Rabbit.* New York: Doubleday, 1958. A delightful story on the power of love to make us real and the price we pay that it may happen.

Teacher Aids

Bettelheim, Bruno. *The Uses of Enchantment*. New York: Random House, 1977.

Chesterton, G.K. *Orthodoxy*. New York: Doubleday, 1973.

Haughton, Rosemary. *Tales from Eternity*. New York: Seabury.

Lane, Belden C. *Story Telling: The Enchantment of Theology* (4 tapes). Minneapolis: Bethany Press, 1982.

Sawyer, Ruth. *The Way of the Storyteller*. New York: Penguin Books, 1977.

Shedlock, Marie L. *The Art of the Story-teller*. New York: Dover Publications.